T0168535

MATERIAL

BY ROS BARBER

How Things Are on Thursday
2004

ROS BARBER
Material

ANVIL PRESS POETRY

Published in 2008
by Anvil Press Poetry Ltd
Neptune House 70 Royal Hill London SE10 8RF
www.anvilpresspoetry.com

This book is published with financial assistance
from Arts Council England

Designed and set in Monotype Bulmer by Anvil
Printed and bound in England
by Cromwell Press, Trowbridge, Wiltshire

ISBN 0 85646 410 2

A catalogue record for this book
is available from the British Library

For my mother, deceased
and my father, living

*Poetry is a way of talking to your loved ones
when it's too late.*

TED HUGHES

Acknowledgements

The writing of this book would not have been possible without financial support from Arts Council England and the Authors' Foundation, both of whom are gratefully acknowledged. Acknowledgements are also due to the editors of the following publications in which some of these poems first appeared: *10/9*, *Magma*, *MsLexia*, *New Welsh Review*, *nthposition*, *Pedestal*, *Poetry London*, *Poetry Review*, *The Second Tall Lighthouse Poetry Review*.

'Flesh and Blood' was a commission for Pallant House Gallery in Chichester, inspired by the following works whose artists should be credited:

> 'Reclining Nude (Vera)' by Matthew Smith (1924)
> 'Shell' by Susie MacMurray (2007)
> 'Hers Is a Lush Situation' by Richard Hamilton (1958)
> 'Self Portrait at Seventy' by Victor Willing (1987)

'Amusements', 'Denizens', 'How to Leave the World that Worships *Should*', 'Out of Season' and 'Stuck' were commissioned by Canterbury City Council as part of the Seaside Sonnets project for Herne Bay. 'Relatively New Development' was commissioned by Wealden District Council. 'Dear Diary' was commissioned by photographer Neville Gabie. 'First Access' was a prize-winner in the Strokestown International Poetry Competition.

Belatedly and in some cases posthumously, the author would like to thank those individuals who supported her in the process of becoming one, including Stephen Baines, Peter Barber, Vivien Davies, Michael Donaghy, Celia Hunt, Peter Jay, Keiren Phelan, Catherine Smith and Paul Stones.

Finally, apologies are due to all those individuals who find themselves incorporated as 'material' when they would have chosen otherwise.

Contents

Missing

Test Series

MATERIAL

Material

My mother was the hanky queen
when hanky meant a thing of cloth,
not paper tissues bought in packs
from late-night garages and shops,
but things for waving out of trains
and mopping the corners of your grief:
when hankies were material
she'd have one, always, up her sleeve.

Tucked in the wrist of every cardi,
a mum's embarrassment of lace
embroidered with a V for Viv,
spittled and scrubbed against my face.
And sometimes more than one fell out
as if she had a farm up there
where dried-up hankies fell in love
and mated, raising little squares.

She bought her own; I never did.
Hankies were presents from distant aunts
in boxed sets, with transparent covers
and script initials spelling *ponce,*
the naffest Christmas gift you'd get –
my brothers too, more often than not,
got male ones: serious, and grey,
and larger, like they had more snot.

It was hankies that closed department stores,
with headscarves, girdles, knitting wool
and trouser presses; homely props
you'd never find today in malls.

Hankies, which demanded irons,
and boiling to be purified
shuttered the doors of family stores
when those who used to buy them died.

And somehow, with the hanky's loss,
greengrocer George with his dodgy foot
delivering veg from a Comma van
is history, and the friendly butcher
who'd slip an extra sausage in,
the fishmonger whose marble slab
of haddock smoked the colour of yolks
and parcelled rows of local crab

lay opposite the dancing school
where Mrs White, with painted talons,
taught us *When You're Smiling* from
a stumbling, out of tune piano:
step-together, step-together, step-together,
point! The Annual Talent Show
when every mother, fencing tears,
would whip a hanky from their sleeve
and smudge the rouge from little dears.

Nostalgia only makes me old.
The innocence I want my brood
to cling on to like ten-bob notes
was killed in TV's lassitude.
And it was me that turned it on
to buy some time to write this poem
and eat bought biscuits I would bake
if I'd commit to being home.

There's never a hanky up my sleeve.
I raised neglected-looking kids,
the kind whose noses strangers clean.
What awkwardness in me forbids
me to keep tissues in my bag
when handy packs are 50p?
I miss material handkerchiefs,
their soft and hidden history.

But it isn't mine. I'll let it go.
My mother too, eventually,
who died not leaving handkerchiefs
but tissues and uncertainty:
and she would say, should I complain
of the scratchy and disposable,
that *this is your material
to do with, daughter, what you will.*

My First Three Children

My first three children aren't like you. They come
from a crippled home where oxygen caught fire
over their heads in a bitter civil war:
they had to breathe the poison they were raised on.

One eats nothing, one as if he's starving.
One's a bomb gone off, one's quiet as rain.
They're sort of broken, battered at in passing
like kitchen furniture. I can explain.

I didn't know how much three children weighed.
Forgot how sound reverberates through walls.
You'll see I fixed this one with Sellotape.
You shouldn't poke the big one when he's bored.
Their scars? Invisible. And yet they pull:
the skin is stronger, but inflexible.

Amusements

This is how it goes: the girl says ah,
the boy imagines he can win her one,
and there, with faces pressed against the glass,
her faith in his perfection is undone:
for after a time the time shows on her face
though, gladiator, he might stay forever
hoping his skill at judging depth and place
will win the toy already bought twice over –

only to watch the bear be pawed and dropped
as gently as a summer fall of snow;
the crane arrive limp-wristed at the top
as though the crane-claw has no muscle tone.
Another token. She has wandered off
to look for something she's allowed to scoff.

Mrs

Suddenly, Mrs: just as you had sketched
a snog of boyfriends' surnames tacked on yours
like patches on the scuffed-out knees of jeans;
a signature you'd have to practise new
and Mrs on the phone: a foreign pause
before you understand the call's for you.

The wedding cards were quick to relish it,
and all the guests who wanted to be first
to call you Mrs Something-else-than-you,
to see you try it on, and say it fits.
A luggage label, *Wife, belonging to:*
Even worn soft, at night, the binding hurts.

And letters, Mrs. Sometimes all his name
both first and last, as if you don't exist
except to be the adjunct to his essence;
except to orbit round him, bland, dismissed,
a shadow of the girl he fell in love with,
who lost a part of her each time she kissed.

It's hard to love her, Mrs. But for months
you'll wear her, chafing, with the other's name
still rubbing at your comfort like a shoe
whose leather hasn't softened. Wear the shame
that adolescent wishes have come true
and obliterated half the words for you.

Sheds

Each garden in view has a shed.
Six by eights, or eight by tens
with miserly windows.
The sheds hunker at the edges
of tight little gardens.
The gardens are identical:

same size, same shape,
same dim hum of green
from the lawn, same prawn-pink
patio slabs, same creosoted
shiplap fences
marking their place

like the bent-down corners
of books that will never be
picked up and read
but will make thought
seem possible, there to be had
when the phone stops ringing,

if the telly wouldn't beg
to be watched. Late at night,
some of the sheds shed light.
Inside, husbands twist and tighten,
do and undo, tinker with things
that aren't broken.

Denizens

The curved glass window holds the tide in place,
the ample bosoms and porridge cardigans.
The counter offers, in their childhood tongue,
Knickerbocker Glory, Butterscotch Sundae, Shakes.
They ruminate, through the tobacco smog,
on sausages smooth as a Hoover salesman's patter –
the shopping trollies like small obedient dogs,
the talk contained at things that barely matter.

These were the sweater girls and Brylcreemed youth
who came here fifty years ago as teens
to heal themselves with cappuccino froth
and shock their parents wearing denim jeans –
the East End waiters suddenly *signores*;
the opulent desserts, quite clearly, glories.

Relatively New Development

They made these roads deliberate dead-ends:
looped them round, and knotted them in bows,
called them cul-de-sacs, as if they're French,
called them flower names, topped off with Close.

Close as the mosses crammed into the cracks
of kerbstones, flying ants in summer plague,
ungreeted neighbours, every one detached.
Close as a city three days' walk away.

Close as the hanging straps that lurch his sleep,
the underarms of strangers, suits of sweat,
the coffee-solid state of *not there yet.*
Close as the single hours she has to keep.

Close as an August overdue its rain,
the metered tap that pumps the flowers alive,
the television shows that hold her sane,
close as the chips of gravel in the drive.

Close as a mobile phone against her thigh,
the vacuumed yawning of an empty day,
the double-glazing gap, its dying fly;
close as a wife whose husband works away.

Close as a train that whistles past his nose,
the end of him just inches from its cliff,
his feelings briefcase-tight inside his ribs.
Close as a man who doesn't know he's close.

Close as a U-turn. Worn-out verges skulk
by sullen drives, and lawns not worth the bother,
while in their plotted quiet, they wait it out,
each wondering what happened to the other.

Bad Mother

She lost their childhoods in a blaze of blues,
of sleep-free nights and irritated days,
a playground mum who couldn't watch them play
and couldn't wait for bedtime, and the booze.

No wonder they'd refuse to go to sleep,
get up, with needs, repeatedly, for hours.

No wonder that they'd never pick her flowers;
or if they did, because they heard her weep;
or sometimes, from a sudden fear that she
would vanish from her misery, and them;
or like a wish, to say *be you again.*

I couldn't look that woman in the eye.
But she, amongst her children's flowers, is dead.
Her kids are mine by pure coincidence.

The Old Ship Hotel

Ten years ago, an early husband stood
behind her shoulder, barking at the moon.
The chambers of his heart were made of wood
that fear of failure petrified. Now stone,
but still that stone was asking for her love;

was asking in a battery of words
that thudded shell-holes deep across the plain
and barren land their misery preferred.
The pounding noise would drive a man insane;
this woman too. And fixed upon the street

she opened the window. January's blast
was cool. The traffic's roar three floors below
mimicked the waves that thundered like a past
one cannot now atone for. Time was slow
like running in nightmare. Answer this:

how did the hotel rear up like a cliff
and have her calculate how far the drop,
whether the fall would lengthen, or be swift,
and what a mess she'd make, seen from the top?
The worst she could imagine: she'd survive,

a helpless cripple in a pushing chair,
a grown-up baby, dribbling from her lips,
the barking man to drive her here and there,
speaking for her. Quite dead below the hips
and angrily alive inside the brain.

Ten years of waking up began at once.
She slipped the latch and left the man alone.
And ten years later she can use her lungs
to thank the air and breathe it as a poem
against the patient breaking of the waves.

Belated Apology

If I brushed your knotted hair when I was angry,
if I let you hear me crying on the phone,
if I snapped at you from underneath a duvet,
or told my friends *I can't bear being alone*
in front of you (if you can still remember),
if I railed at you in pure hypocrisy,
accusing you of being in a temper
when you were only trying to be like me –

sorry. Here's my apology. I never
expected my longed-for baby long ago
to become a thing whose growing made it heavier
to hip-walk to the car, another load

when all the shopping wasn't in; a yell
I couldn't stomach, being starved myself.

The Means

Inhabit this: you're eight years old.
One parent who loved you is traded in
for a tooth whistle and a frown of gold.
The other, who stays, is catering
for a new house head, a man of tin.
No room for you between the hands they hold,
the hands they kiss, the hands they swing
and the lovers' laughter has a ring
like silence when the will unfolds.

Step into children hated by
the man who needs their mother more.
Imagine where her safety lies.
It isn't you, with your fold-out horse,
your messed-up head, your snapped *Of course,*
the look that stabs her in the eye.
She really didn't have a choice;
good women cannot stay divorced
and no-one wants to see you cry.

Put this on top: you get to eat
exactly what your mum affords
while new step-siblings twice a week
are lavished with meat, a second course.
Daily he butters up his toast
while you gag on cooking margarine.
This raw dessert: it isn't yours.
Barred from the sweets you love the most,
you're forced to steal the gold-top cream.

You fill your stomach in the fields
when strawberry-picking days have come,
knowing you'll be served up last
and left the purple, squashy ones.
But the fact the cream is also gone,
the dregs of Devon's milking farms
too weak to trespass from the jug,
and nothing shared out fairly, once –
that sticks in your throat like a baby's arm.

Your nightmares, now, consist of queues
where others come away well-fed
with mountain trays of food, while you,
the last in line, are given bread.
And those who seem to wish you dead?
It suits them that you get upset,
the lump in your throat preventing speech;
that you get quieter week by week –
you'd only say something they'd regret.

So do you feel like an orphan yet?
Do love and food now smell the same?
Are there barbecues you can't forget
for the way they set your cheeks aflame
as you tried to prove your worth again,
your value above economy brands?
Your parents left you choking bones,
a third class citizen of home,
and not entitled to the jam.

DRIVING WITHOUT LIGHTS

Bones

Without his love to feed upon, she couldn't eat.
If no-one cared then she would not care too.
So coffee was her saline, black and pointless,
and cigarettes her substitute for meat.
And lovers settled down to share their pastries
or ate each other's faces in the street.

Without a lover's appetite to cook for, she closed
her mouth and left her tongue to sleep alone.
So her bones whistled, and men ran up like dogs
to sniff her marrow, close to being exposed.
And none of them were lovers who might feed her.
Their only real interest was in bones.

Losing It

She's not like the people who lose their dogs
by driving to Wales and opening the door.

She's like the people who lose their phones
in swimming pools, against hard floors,
or into the pockets of handbag thieves,
while the owner was ordering something to eat.

She's not like the people who lose their wives
with a rope, and a hammer, and a carving knife.

She's like the people who lose their way home
with a belly full of vodka on a dark night
two weeks after moving to Poet's Name Road
off something or other. Around here, though.

She's not like the people who lose their lovers
by forgetting dates, and screening calls.

She's like the people who lose a limb,
are haunted by dreams of what it's for
and feel its ache as though it's there,
thick with the uselessness of air.

She's not like the people who lose their shirt
on a worthless nag in the three-fifteen.

She's like the people who lose hope
through a hole in the lining of a favourite coat
though they'd put their name on the thing okay,
and were sure they had it yesterday.

She's not like the people who go on a diet.
She's like the people who starve on the quiet.

She Exists

The scales still notice she exists.
Mornings slash their wrists
to sorry light
and tip her into numbers:
stones like castles,
pounds like fists.

But food has forgotten her name,
the deli delights silently ashamed
they can't remember knowing
this doll of pure denial,
her hips so slim
they don't disturb the air.

Sunlight still wants to see her,
blanks the transparent
so the shops are dipped
in mirrors she slides past
broken, admiring
the beauty of nothing.

But hunger has moved to another town
with another woman
who needed him more,
and his guilty heart
and his secret stash
of her letters.

Driving Without Lights

Dark road. Not even moonlight
spilling its ministry over the lip
of the kerb, and she switches off.

Tyres gasp, hug tarmac
as cat's-eyes close,
blinding the corners.

This thin, she could go anywhere.
Halve the breath between
oncoming juggernauts, slip

between atoms, the rapid alarm
of her pulse beating her back to a past
where she couldn't be good enough.

Now she's a wonder,
miraculously missing
the things she can't see:

looming verges snapped off
like safety tabs, pylons scarpered,
rabbits invisible sentinels

in the black of the land.
Regular telegraph poles
her waist is smaller than

swish past in the dark
like the hated days.
She's fast.

Until her eyes adjust
nothing can touch her.
She's put out existence.

Home Visit

Existence happens, tick by tick,
no matter what she'd rather.
Her mother's sofa, where she'd sleep
if thought would have enough of her

and drop her from its busy jaws.
The distance of her father
who hugs her to his laundered chest:
a bucket lowered down a well.

A delicate creature, carted home,
whose habits are nocturnal.
The brandy goes. She stands and shivers
back-door smokes. When daylight comes

she makes an exhibition of
pretending to be normal
to Mother Guilt and Father Fear,
who made her something, pity them,

and sank in her the need for love,
a deeper need than breathing.
At six a.m. she takes the car.
She parks it on the promenade

a blurry twenty miles away.
Her anger isn't leaving:
it loiters at the kitchen door
and waits for scraps that rarely come.

Her face is blame, they want her gone,
and she won't disappoint them;
will disappear from where they taught
the endless appetites of love.

The Weight of Ink

She had to give him up. He didn't want her.
The phone was quiet as Christmas, and the snow
was coming thick as torn-off scraps of paper
he hadn't thought to cross his kisses on.

She had to give him up. Her only pleasure
– appearing in the full-length mirror, nude –
could not uplift the ballast of her insides:
a molten black, the rotting of a clam.

She had to give him up. She had to give him
nothing, to remind him of their love:
and her, the wailing car that's broken into,
gone silent with the battery run down.

She had to give him up. She wrote a letter
on the lightest airmail paper she could find,
and walked it to the postbox like a prisoner,
the weight of ink disgraceful in her hand.

A Simple Cure

A boy cat, black, castrated please.
She's chipper at the rescue home.
He's hungry for her love, this one;
knuckles his skull against her palm.

But on the backseat, in a box,
he's threatening as the darkened look
some violent husbands shoot their wives.
She tells herself it's just a cat.

She tells him, *you're the only male*
who'll share my bed from this day on.
He glowers like the stupid things
she wrote to stop from going mad.

The first night, when she comes to bed,
he's on her pillow like a rose
that won't be moved. A blur of thorns.
As soon as she feels her hand stung red,

the curse she should have saved for men
who hurt before they understood her,
shears the flowers from bedroom walls;
the cat, a novice, learns to fly.

If she weren't empty, she would cry.
There's nothing left to give the cat.
Just Kitekat. It's practical.
She strokes the bastard. Eats some bread.

The Caretaker

You're very thin, the new man says,
kissing reluctance down to skin.
She's embarrassed for her shrunken breasts.
It took her months to let him in

and still he's held just at the gate:
even when she seems to give,
the living part of her is safe,
its treasure locked inside her chest.

And the man that isn't there, is there,
lodged at the front like a concierge,
oblivious to the draughts from doors
whose seals he was engaged to fix.

Her body, white, unfolds its map,
her veins blue roads to Broken Down:
the new man's heard the tales of that
unravelled over emptied cups

and knows he won't be living there,
a town of ghosts and kicked-in doors,
its shutters banging in the wind,
its gold rush over. He'll take talk

more open than he has at home,
her blackened jokes. He'll take her chin
and lift it, saying honestly,
'You're safe. I don't expect a thing.'

And the man that isn't there, is there,
the trace of his damage written on her
like clever letters under glass:
you have to understand, to pass.

Afterwards, he holds her close.
The rattling of a train of doubts
expressed across her bedroom left
the fixtures swinging. Lovers, still.

No rush, he says. Her ear on his heart,
logging the slowing thump of blood,
astonished at how suddenly love
falls on the man prepared to wait.

And the man that isn't there's not there:
for the first time in a death-long year
she doesn't summon up his face,
unfold his name; the vacant chair's

already put out on the street.
It's kisses that she hungers for.
The no-man's-land her mouth became,
filled with a good and honest tongue.

FLESH AND BLOOD

Reclining Nude (Vera)

Vera Cunningham, artist, was Matthew Smith's
mistress and model

Some afternoons, our palettes side by side,
desire made it hard to concentrate.
The muse, insistent ache beguiled to bed,
allows the artist's tongue and skin and flesh
to make her feel. After, he'd paint me red
as the blush of love he'd drawn up through my skin,
let love quicken the ballet of his hands
flattering brush through loosened oils, begin
to work with the passion I had grown in him.

He stands where the window lights me best. He groans
but cannot stop to kiss me, for the glow
of the Paris afternoon is leaving swiftly:
red will be grey, the velvet cushions shadowed,
the gold knocked from their nap like jilted wives.
This man undoes me, and I'm thrilled to let him;
art is an anchor shored against forgetting,
and pleasure fades as quickly as the light.
So neither of us thinks about tomorrow.

But here you are, and staring at my breasts,
deliciously in public view, preserved
like summer cherries in a Kilner jar.
My name in brackets, I'm *Reclining Nude*,
mistress and model. Artist once, but now
I'm mostly naked flesh on canvas. Who,
which woman, wouldn't want to be a muse,

be loved and painted, courted, and adored.
And yet. I spent myself as artist's fuel.
Not quite anonymous, an almost cruel
illusion of breath, and breathlessness, and blood.

Shell

Gone now, though the memory is here:
an absence on the wide, waxed flight of stairs,
a nudity half-panelled to the chest,
and silence measured by a hallway clock
whose habit knocks anxiety from air.

A feast of empties echoed hungry mouths
that shucked the flesh from violated shell:
the snapped-shut wife prised open night on night,
the gory feasting she could live without,
the blood-red velvet intimate as hell.

You can cut yourself on a mussel: black and blue –
the oily ink of waters late at night
that swallow sailors put to sleep by drink;
a wife who dreams of how he'd slip and sink,
the knuckles that struck her blurring with decay.

The wealth of love wasted between these walls
curses the air to leave the hall bewitched,
the heart's long muscle slippered into two,
the stairs she dreaded to ascend now shadowed
by twenty thousand pairs of broken lips.

Hers Is a Lush Situation

All she has left are her lips, enticing,
lips made for kissing, no delicate dab
of the napkin, no talking, no teething,
no mouthing to wits who won't listen,
no audible breathing

except under bedclothes
seeming to love him,
lips soft as an unconscious kitten
in need of desire,
alone as ambition,

she floats over chrome and curve, lips
slightly open, unpicked from her skin
like a scab. Hardly broken, she's gone,
her substance erased not by age
but the speed of the age. Lips,

their colour, old bacon;
revered beyond using and tinged
with the green of not being taken;
blood stagnating to verdigris kiss
and brown smear on the wing.

Self-Portrait at Seventy

Sky blue as a boyhood thick
with lazy, laid-back summers,
wispless July chewing on grass-stems
and dreams of girls in open blouses;
blue as perfection, as birdfree
and cloudless, lung-deep in wonder.

Or blue as a sky tormenting a desert
baked down to crumbs of a biscuit, a relic,
blue of a fierce god's gaze whose subjects
jug themselves into succulent tubers,
gecko-run over the heat, retreat
into burrows, grow useless.

Or blue as a soft-brushed blanket;
curtains of rooms where boy babies suckle,
their mothers their harbours,
their fathers their anchors;
blue shielding the gender and art
of a new human being.

Or blue as the flash that unsettles the houses
and turns off discreetly on reaching your street
to stretcher the body with eyes you could see through –
all the way through to the blessings of heaven –
the soul reduced to a blip on a read-out,
this human soon to be no longer being.

MISSING

How to Leave the World that Worships *Should*

Let faxes butter-curl on dusty shelves.
Let junk mail build its castles in the hush
of other people's halls. Let deadlines burst
and flash like glorious fireworks somewhere else.
As hours go softly by, let others curse
the roads where distant drivers queue like sheep.
Let e-mails fly like panicked, tiny birds.
Let phones, unanswered, ring themselves to sleep.

Above, the sky unrolls its telegram,
immense and wordless, simply understood:
you've made your mark like birdtracks in the sand –
now make the air in your lungs your livelihood.
See how each wave arrives at last to heave
itself upon the beach and vanish. Breathe.

No Wonder Caroline Bites People

Since someone didn't check their rear-view mirror,
since brain hit skull as hard as car hit bike,
since nine months' sleep through fear she can't remember
except for shattered words she didn't like,

she hasn't been the same. Her legs are spastic.
Her speech is slurred as an idiot's on gin.
Her right hand does a Captain Hook impression
since someone slammed the brakes and left her in

a fleshy cage, with most of the controllers
dummied like a baby's dashboard box,
or taped in one position: like a lighthouse
that's spinning dark, a spanner in the cogs.

She hasn't got a handshake, or a whistle,
a sexy pout, an air kiss, or a wink.
She has got limbs that don't obey her wishes
and carers to make sure she doesn't stink,

to wash her face, to help her with her toilet,
to have a word with onlookers who stare,
to feed her on the days she can't be bothered,
to help her put her feet up on a chair –

like Emperors of Rome. Like Princess Gaa-Gaa.
Like all the crippled *petits saints* of Lourdes.
And like the rest of us, she has her good days:
is glad, at least, the driver was insured.

So sit and watch her disobedient finger
trail trembled swear words on her spelling board
(forgo the joyful violence of delivery:
the plosives on her lips, her vocal chords

vibrating with the pleasure of a *bastard*).
And when you see her, bow in Caroline's praise.
For she's got brains. And able-bodied carers
to sink her teeth into on crappy days.

Out of Season

Like a titled youth whose guests have gone
a cormorant airs his underarms
on the sign that says 'Beware Soft Mud' –
his shabby dinner suit undone.
And now no-one's around to hear,
the warbled tune from the arcade
– *If you go down to the woods today* –
is rather getting on in years.

The clock tower calls and no-one comes.
The sea-forts bloom like mushrooms on
the mackerel line. There's herring in.
And only the faithful, quiet as sin,
give thanks to the god of seaside towns.
A seat. A sky that won't shut down.

Girls' High Empties

Their blouses, the hours of a dandelion clock
blown in breaths from double doors.
Puffs of them soften the gate in clots
or clog up the road they shouldn't cross –
none of them looking, none of them yours:
drifts of girls, their legs held up by socks.

Bottle-green blazers, fingers bruised with blue
and all their sunlit lips unhurt by kisses, blow
by blow, blow past the boy without a clue,
who just for a second dreams he isn't you –
and almost look, but no – and on they go.
It's agony to stand here, but you do.

And then they're gone, like summer shuttered out,
bouquets thrown gently into each other's homes,
to comb their hair and let their legs out long,
and long, long after, you'll be hanging on
with the frozen hope that one of them might, alone,
come back this way for something she forgot.

The Women

Tell it softly, how the women slept
with all they owned beneath their heads,
the curl of daughters where their men had been;
and how the dark infested everything –

midnight strolling calm through the noon street,
shadows at home, the meat congealed,
the goat's milk in its bucket turning black.
How, at dawn, only the crows clapped.

The bread shucked off from lorries,
left in heaps. At the edge of the forest
someone's newborn cried itself cold.
The sun hung in the air like stone.

The right and the wrong words were gone.
Now no-one spoke as they bent, one by one
at the standpipe, and touched life lightly at the tap
in the hope it might not touch them back.

Millennium Eve

Not any New Year. The one she'd counted to
since she first thought of it, at seven or eight;
the night she'd finally meet the future self
who'd be in love, and almost thirty-six.

A confluence. A joy to be conscious when
so few witness the numbers come aligned –
like watching dad's old Renault clock the speedo
and feeling warmed by one big row of noughts.

Not any New Year. The one she'd had in mind
when each New Year before it fell to shreds
of burst balloons, and people that don't love you
but say they do until their friends arrive.

A moment's respite: like the false relief
of being released from chaos into calm;
like halting for an instant on a fright-ride
and thinking that's the worst it's going to get.

Not any New Year. The one the government planned,
that councils planted parks for, village funds
raised sculptured towers to celebrate; its coming
exploding history over public squares.

A necessary fiction. Half the planet
singing drunk in parties under clocks,
their arms linked in a temporary rescue
to pull them from the quicksand of themselves.

Not any New Year. The one where she'd be struck
by all the beauty of a world now hers;
mistakes complete and suddenly last century
and he, the one, would be on hand to kiss.

For time to put your problems in perspective,
for one split second, life to fall in line …
but midnight comes, and no-one's there to kiss you,
and someone grabs and swallows your champagne,

and *Happy New Year!* shout a thousand voices
though through your tears not one of them is yours,
and only the numbers 2, and 1, and zero
mean anything to those in midnight's arms.

A thousand years of pitiless improvement.
Fireworks pounding happiness in the sky.
Your champagne bottle dancing with a stranger.
The man you love, elsewhere, has kissed his wife.

First Access

Sometimes, in my dreams, he brings them back.
Three blond toddlers, born of what they like
to call a 'stormy relationship', like a fair fight.
But he was the lightning; me, the sapling struck.
I was young: I thought love fierce and desperate.
I knew no better until our first was born.
That was love. And I didn't understand
how love can suckle quietly at your breast,
and later, throw you downstairs by your hair.

But I forgave him: once blond boy himself,
whose father whipped a belt across his thighs
for misdemeanours. Swung him by the legs
for buying ice-cream with a bob he found.
Punched him into fractures, just for being.
If he thought love was darkness, could you blame him?
He'd crumple and cry, like he was six years old
until I found forgiveness, which he used
like a rag to mop the evidence away.

II

Sometimes, in my dreams, he brings them back.
They tumble off to rooms I haven't tidied,
where mismatched toys are frozen in the act
of telling important stories: picnics, rescues,
battles where Good will out-manoeuvre Evil.
They say *this one's the daddy*, watch him bash
the Lego castle into bits that won't

be built again, the Barbie mummy trapped
inside a crumbling home she should have left.

I should have left. A thousand times. I know.
Before the kids. Or after the umpteenth night
he split a lip, or broke a tooth, or cracked
my head against the plaster. But he knew.
That I was small and worthless, not worth loving;
that only *he* could love me, since the curse
of being raised by normal, fucked-up parents.
Every time, I dredged up my forgiveness.
And every time, it only made things worse.

III

Sometimes, in my dreams, he brings them back.
They're almost as they are in photographs;
except alive, of course. But something's wrong.
I can't say what it is. A smell, like dawn
still miles from a lay-by's dark: the absent sunlight
frigid on their clothes. Their skin, tinged with
the lightest blue, detergent-white. They're spooked,
as if they passed themselves; the other version,
where three blond boys are sleeping in a car.

Sorry. You know, it never goes away.
I *live* to have those dreams: I sleep, and sleep,
and drug myself to stay there, in the hope
the door will ring and here they are again,
into my arms like lambs into the fold.
I don't look up. I know he's standing there,
his anger like a tumour of the heart,
and how he almost wants congratulations
for not, this time, dealing the fatal blow.

Dear Diary

It's not that I don't have a friend.
My friends exist. They called today.
I couldn't say a word to them,
they filled me up. What would you say
(and would you dare speak up again)
if all your friends had glass in them,
were made of glass, or moved away?
Or just glazed over before the end?

Dear Diary, when I talk to you,
I don't know who's on the other side
of the black cloth. But it's you I choose
to run my dumb ambitions by.
I think of you as an older me
familiar with my reality:
forgive me as I prophesise
the history of your family.

So, shared between the sort that feel:
here's something heard, or something said.
Dear Diary, as if you're real,
as if you have a heart and head,
I stuff my feelings into you,
fly-tip my capital letters too,
rather than take their spikes to bed
like occupying forces do.

I'm flooded, you're the hired pump
whose sucking draws the mud away;
the out-of-earshot rubbish dump
where mortar-stricken children play

and fish for scraps they'll sell for bread;
you're my amanuensis, head
of every heart that you survey;
you make sense of the sorry mess.

And you'll be anyone I want:
the mother I felt abandoned by,
the former love I hope looks on,
the chalklines where the body lies
for hours before we make it art,
and with your help I'll take apart
or apprehend (and undisguise)
the criminals who stole my heart.

And I can rely on you not to scoff
when whole battalions, boys or men,
are written in, then out, then off:
the talking cure meets ballpoint pen.
You're the bunker; this is war.
You talk me through the toilet door
and help me face the crowds again.
But that's not what I keep you for.

You're the safe deposit box that stows
her bitching, his philandering;
the leather-bound couch where I unload
my words like laundry, wondering
if that makes me a basket case,
forever scratching at your face
emotional pirates plundering
a member of the feeling race.

When we get older, we'll count daffs;
I'll note the year without regret
and catalogue my photographs.
And you will play my oubliette.
And one day you'll say *look at me*,
and a sorted, older you will see
the secret book of unsent letters
you wrote because you couldn't speak.

Ventriloquist

The voice is yours. Ventriloquist,
I borrowed it. I don't know how
it ended up in the wrong suitcase
crooning mid-Atlantic vowels,
an elegance of incantation
soft beneath the stolen towels.

There was me repeating spells,
that wisdom from another age,
the trick I picked up quietly
from watching you behind the stage
pulling a patter of scarves and mirrors
from a non-existent page;

there was me, alone, wrapped up
in words that make the light appear,
the puff of smoke in which we palm
our thoughts like coins from someone's ear,
when presto! It was *your* voice spoke,
and like a genie's wish, you're here.

Perhaps I've read too many books.
When inspiration goes too far,
perhaps we breathe the other in?
A voice is half of what we are.
Perhaps I summoned up your spirit,
chanting verses in the dark.

It didn't pass from lip to lip
that night in a frozen seaside town
when we found we'd got ahead of them,
but love, offshore, was bearing down
and I was afraid I couldn't swim,
so we didn't kiss. I'd rather drown

in the book-logged words you left behind
than miss your lips, your skin, your touch.
My compensation is your voice.
And though I'm scarred and lightning-struck,
in every window candles burn.
The art is not to say too much.

We were not lovers. Friend, we shared
not words of love, but love of words.
I never knew your house or wife.
To write to you this way's absurd
except that you possess my head;
your voice, a familiar purr that stirs
a heart I didn't dare to hurt
to send me poems from the dead.

Nocturnal

The unwritten poems his wife thinks of as vermin
scratch and chew inside his head all night,
stripping each sentence free of its connectives,
their vision better than she'd like to think.
The softened fall of rhyme, they use as bedding;
each noun and verb, they squirrel into store;
extended metaphors, they try to hide in ...
he listens, while his wife arranges bait.

And only by ignoring them on purpose
and saying they don't bother him these days
will his wife put down the scimitar of her slipper,
the heavy book she'd like to meet the floor
with all the poems under, squashed to titles.
Especially the ones he'd write to *Her*.

What Blue Is

A character's name in all those films that flopped.
The road signs for the motorway cafés
he sits in, writing nothing. Smoke nooses
that used to side-wind from his father's pipe.

The ocean's helplessness on perfect days.
The ink of schoolgirl fingers pressed against
the bare V of his schoolboy chest. Her face
when lights were out, and parents coming home.

The gentle poison of an old tattoo.
The chlorinated pools of movie stars
he may have dreamed of kissing. All the songs
of Billie Holliday. What else is blue?

His mother's sapphire ring. Fifth chakra, throat.
His shirts, since they were bought by her, his wife.
Her frosted eyelids when she's going out;
the coat he drives her to auditions in.

The tell-tale kissing of a recent bruise.
The menu screen. The oxygen-poor blood
in the right of his heart. The woman he used to call,
when he was partly hers, and she all his,

under the lie of having to move his car;
her language when he left her all alone
to curse herself; the shadows of the flowers
his mother picked to decorate the church

where he would marry guilt. A passing van.
A sky that every summer throws at him
for stopping short and giving in; the thought
that sky is not a thing, but emptiness;

what isn't there is blue. The sugar wrap.
The cup he gets his second coffee in.
That thing she used to wear. The final draft,
when he can almost taste what he has lost.

Stuck

This town's like you. It seems a gentle scrap
modernity couldn't finish, and pushed aside.
Its dated haircuts nod from barbershops.
Its half-cocked smiling won't quite meet my eye.
A softer thing that doesn't know the rules
and blindly adds its sweetness to my cup.
A pace that slows – as though my watch were stopped –
until the raindrops hang themselves like jewels.

And flies, like stitches snipped from healing wounds,
fall here to sip the glitter of the sap;
to tend our broken tenderness in tombs
so softly set we cannot know we're trapped.
An amber light. The rest of life, remote.
It's love, my love, that catches at the throat.

Missing

Someone loved went missing
and the town caved in.
Waiters stormed from restaurants,
ladies drank gin

neat as folded handkerchiefs
before they filled the street
and crumpled into lily blossoms
littered at our feet.

Diaries were emptied,
people took the stairs,
and no-one dared to breathe the air
in case it wasn't theirs.

Teachers cried in staff rooms,
doctors took to bed,
telephones were wrung from walls,
letters lay unread,

and all the life we couldn't stand
was swallowed like a pill.
A town called Acceptance,
population: nil.

*

Someone loved went missing
and the shopfronts shut,
flowered with graffiti
exposing its *but*

so we couldn't buy a paper,
and wouldn't want to read
a thousand other towns like ours
had not been so bereaved.

No-one's loss as big as ours,
no-one's as keen,
and no-one that we recognised
where once our love had been.

No-one cared what happened next
so everyone went home.
Women turned to water.
Men turned to stone.

Siblings turned to alcohol
and wearing out their shoes.
A town called Acceptance,
home of the blues.

*

Someone loved went missing
and we learnt to endure.
Constellations circled
round the sky untracked.

The moon built up and melted:
a candle in the neck
of all our bottled emptiness.
What could we expect

but sobbing from the children's rooms,
the dissonance of loss,
its sorrow drifting sorry miles
across the fields of frost.

And very little else was heard.
Mothers wept alone.
Silence wrapped like bandages
around the wounded homes

whose sleep was broken up by ghosts
or endless hours awake.
A town called Acceptance:
rumour, or fake.

*

Someone loved went missing
and we learnt to endure,
the glass fronts of our porches
looking faintly insecure

and frightened of the gentle chink
as midnight lifts the latch.
The word is always *missing*,
as if they might be back.

But we're the ones left missing,
with bits of us lopped off,
or not at home, or shut up with
the photos in the loft.

The key is on the inside.
A coat is on the rack.
You only have to see that there's
no art to wearing black

and step into the clueless light
of ever-burning sun.
A town called Acceptance,
population: one.

Wrabness

We buried you at Easter: senseless flowers
nailed into what passed as soil in March,
and new thorns throbbing under the bark
of may awakening in the hedgerows.

It was wrong: the sky, bizarrely blue,
the skylark doodling his summer tune
across the blank of what was missing, you.
And you not here to tell us what to do.

Listen.

As though we'd hired his lonely throat –
a soloist in the meadow's open church –
the flavour of love was scribbled across
the cuffing wind. As mourners turned to go

we withstood it, spring's mistimed hello,
and rebirth spread across the land
like post-war margarine: bland,
in poor taste, and an unlikely yellow.

The Recovered

They open mail and answer calls.
They water plants and phone the vet.
They look as if they're functioning,
as if they've hope. They haven't yet.

They pay the bills and brush their teeth.
They feed the cat and clean the car.
They wipe the children's hands and faces,
not okay. You think they are.

You'd never tell them from the rest.
They queue in shops like you and me
to buy the stuff they didn't want,
can nearly concentrate to read

and almost sleep five hours a night.
Will take the weather as it comes.
From time to time they laugh at films;
at least, the darkly funny ones.

If they were fully better, they'd
be flippant with their birthday wish.
And not write poems in the dark.
And never need to finish this.

TEST SERIES

Maiden Innings

How you loved the cricket,
trailing it with you from room to room
on your coffee-and-cream Bush Radio whose antenna,
straining for the long wave in the kitchen,
tapped our bare legs as we traipsed to the fridge
for the watered-down juice of home-made ice-lollies.

Cricket: the distant *knock*;
the silence of an unseen crowd admiring an arc;
polite applause – all goodness and manners
preserved in an oval of sanity.
The comments of gentlemen over
a good cup of tea and home-made cake.

The Englishness of Rain Stopped Play,
tea declared the moment things go wrong.
Botham running in from the Nursery End,
an umpire's nod is granted like a wish –
the radio coverage of cricket
is proof our goodness still exists.

You secured a ribbon of it
up and down stairs, between the floors.
Integrity. A world where people clap
the manners of a man; are all *good sports*.
You swung its signal, room to room:
hand luggage, your portable sense of home.

Through cricket, you'd survive this sped-up time,
a jolt that threw you bodily back as the Seventies
hijacked Progress from the hippies

and put its foot down, reckless.
Women wore swimsuits.
Then babes wore bikinis.

Fifties England signalled from the harbour,
from cheery photo albums, matinées;
its hair and clothes, morality and values,
through storage, leached of colour in the box,
its onceness in the diction of a childhood
when every man in London wore a hat.

Yes, you laughed, *That's how it was, back then.*
The men wore hats. Your Nanna wore hats and gloves.
Doilies and tea cosies, twin beds for the married.
And then you'd say, loud as you'd sing Jerusalem,
not caring if the silence dropped its pint: *I was*
twenty-three! And I'd never seen a penis in my life!

When you stayed up late at college, you drank
cocoa. Men expressed devotion before the kiss,
and after too. They stuttered polite proposals
to a nice girl from a semi in Gant's Hill.
That's practically East London now, you told me.
Though you remembered, still, when there were fields;

your grandad was a gasman with a donkey.
Look, let's stop there. Before we find ourselves
imprisoned by *eight blackjacks for a penny*.
Not all new things are bad: there's calculators.
A box that sets your telly up for rudimentary ping-pong.
Though nothing beats cricket, and Brian Johnston.

You were an all-rounder. Now it's my turn.
Your early dismissal has brought me
to the crease in borrowed flannels
(yours, and once your Dad's). The hush
as the ball leaves the bowler's fingers
sounds like your held breath in the pavilion.

Here's the swing. And woe betide the fielders
whose hats are just to shade them from the sun.
Recall those afternoons where fortunes turned
in the crackle of poor reception. You'd often
sense, amongst those forced to follow on,
a certain recklessness. They'd nothing to lose.

First Man Out

L.G. Hayward 07/02/1907–26/01/1970

He doesn't have a moustache in the photos,
but he had one once, the furry, tickling kiss
was his: my mental scrapbook of your father
reduced to one goodnight when we were kids.

Here, clean-shaved in Fiji, draped in flowers,
villagers fêting those who came by ship.
And here, an on-board bash in dinner jackets,
his eyebrows wild, but nothing on his lip.

That world cruise, six months in '69,
was all he managed. Retired from a job
it was a blessing he'd survived: briefly free
of the London smogs so thick they'd carry off

the wheezing sort, already prone to cough,
like Grandad with the scrapy, half-shot lung
a wartime exercise gone wrong had left;
a chest too weak to hang insurance on.

Sick, not sick of life – that's why the booze,
to cover up the wheeze inside the laugh.
The Reaper waits at home: you stay out late.
A meal with friends, brandy, a good cigar.

After a lunch date with some friends in Stoke,
your mother snoozing, Grandad at the wheel,
he chose an empty road: the new M6.
An evening doorbell brought you two police.

No-one was prepared. And you, the least.
Dad stayed with us; you travelled up alone,
were handed his wallet, glasses, the car radio
the police removed to stop it being stolen –

this the detail that my dad remembers,
the lurching oddity that makes it yours.
You brought it home as if it were his ashes.
As if you'd plug it in and find his voice.

The Corridor of Uncertainty

The corridor of uncertainty is a notional narrow area on and
just outside a batsman's off stump. If a delivery is in the corridor,
it is difficult for a batsman to decide whether to leave the ball, play
defensively or play an attacking shot.

     – WIKIPEDIA, List of cricket terms

Sometimes there isn't a safety shot.
I think of the daughter gone up to Keele
to formally identify
the corpse she can't believe is real.
She has to sign the paperwork.
Do whatever others ask.
Is asked to remove all trace of him,
her most reliable source of love,
and, trailing her husband to his work,
to leave the country. Move abroad.
You'd hated America before.
But maybe California's coast,
its weather and uncertainties,
would help you now. Perhaps the sun
could lick you into shape again,
the balcony in Lafayette
burning the pallor out of you.
All year skies as blue as plates,
hummingbirds on our breakfast porch
whose spectral feathers beat away
the sight of your father in the morgue.
You could almost believe him still at home;
the voice you missed, at the end of unmade
calls across the ocean. Absence
drowned with all the volume of
God Bless America, home of the free;

the land where television shouts.
You never liked the one-way screen.
You'd turn off everything, step out
and brace yourself beneath the sun,
grateful that silence couldn't breach
your afternoons: the rasp of crickets
filling any gaps in speech,
hushing the grasses, tough and blond.
You slept in nothing but the warmth,
sunlight sloshing through every pore,
as if the melted gilt of it
could coat, commemorate, Before.

Two things always stuck with me –
stories I understood you by.
First: the young bride sobbing to sleep
on her wedding night, on honeymoon, told
as she goes to hold her husband's hand,
we don't need to do that anymore,
we're married, dear. Then: twelve years on,
come back from Keele without your Dad,
his working, pristine radio
(a piece of wreckage) in your bag,
you crept into the darkened bed,
exhausted, bursting into tears.
Why are you crying? my father said.
Why are you crying? as if the years
had put a stranger in his skin.
You leapt out of bed, and met your shadow
screaming to be taken in.
And he was no ogre. He was just
raised quiet. Men of my father's sort
are rare as butter in a school
canteen. They'll take your kerbside, guarding

you from splashes. They'll love you perfect,
king beside your queen. But they'll never
wipe the teardrops from your lashes,
or have an inkling what those teardrops
mean. You stepped out of yourself.

You and I might sometimes have
what other people call hysterics.
Why are you crying? my father said.
He wanted to know. He worked in specifics;
a scientist, a man of quantum
cause and effect, of splitting matter
to its smallest particles to get at
the essence of it. He had to be sure.
But that night, and that thing he said,
winkled you open like tinned peaches
under a scout knife, raw as cheeks.
And how could a child understand
the vacuum left by your father's death
that sucked us from our home like air?
And how could a cracking mother explain
why we flew home on a separate plane?
I only understood it late,
after the fag burns on the arms,
the men that hung around like ghouls,
or wriggled away like drowning worms,
after the twenty years of hate
negotiating fatal turns,
the vain attempts to drink neat gin,
only after years of this
did I feel how similar we were,
forged in the nights I sobbed to sleep
when no-one came to tuck me in.

Twelfth Man

Captain. Of course, you were the captain.
Not well behaved enough to be Head Girl,
but keen-to-blisters, sporty: see the photos.
We know the school athletics team was yours.

You're sixty at the family reunion,
still playing tennis weekly with 'The Girls',
still cycling on a bike with racing handles,
and swimming once a day in outdoor pools.

Delighted in your offspring and their children:
enough, you find, to make two cricket teams,
and all the couples keen to play each other.
Don't moan! addressed to single-parent me.

I'm black with grief. The man I love gets married
three weeks from now to someone he forgets,
and this weekend, as your dismal, broken daughter,
I've come to sleep. You tut my cigarettes.

I've come to write in notebooks in the corners,
to get as drunk as common sense forbids;
abandon rooms for fields, in search of silence
and somewhere I can cry unseen by kids.

My children are relieved to find a family
with time for sports besides Destroy Yourself,
and jump around, excited to be chosen,
as, expertly, you divvy to the twelfth.

It's just like school. The order starts to matter
when numbers dwindle to the dregs. Then two.
And standing by a step-niece, she is chosen:
a six-year-old in glasses, over you.

Over me, that is. And I'm not over it.
You're four years dead and still I bleat the tune:
that I had bitterness to keep me sober,
could field or swing a bat as well as you.

Went on to prove it, angrily, with sixes
to count against you: balls of great offence
that needed fishing, soggy, from the water
by 'Uncle Jimbob' wading in his pants.

Later, I couldn't stomach understanding
and escaped the cheerful dinner for a smoke.
You locked me accidentally in the garden.
How odd, my hurt at hearing the back door bolt.

Of course you shut me out. I *was* the darkness.
Camouflaged to my thoughts, more black than glum.
What sat alone at midnight in the garden
was a terror you had never overcome.

Flashback to one summer, us as children
in a storm-tossed open boat, crossing to Sark.
You cheer the cliff-high waves like it's a fair ride.
Force us to ignore the threatening dark;

a dark that I now trailed around like litmus
to test the acid quality of speech,
was flapping from the roof of burning daughter
in rescue signals way beyond your reach,

was dragging through the joy of your reunion
as dirty as a coat along the road
you'd seen your future on. And you'd avoided,
swerving to the bright side, fast and hard.

A dark that took your father in an instant:
a daylight crash, no other car involved;
his glorious daughter pinned for vivisection,
your patent imperfections picked at, cold.

A dark that, in your thirties, stalked your marriage,
admitted you to have your stomach pumped,
and echoed down a car park under Essex
the sound of perfect housewife being dumped.

A dark that took my brother, almost adult,
having hung around his X-rays for a year;
and only marathons would shake it off you,
the shadow on your buried son's all-clear.

Captain. Who else would be the captain?
Who else but you deserved to choose the team?
To bat on your side required a sense of survival.
Of conquering love. Not the bad light of me.

Silly Point

Silly *refers to any fielding position that is located very close
to the batsman.*
  – Common Cricket Terminology, www.abcofcricket.com

Know how I heard about you? I was driving home.
In your dusk, seven hours ahead of mine,
you crossed the road. A truck, parked at the kerb:
a boy of sixteen waits for his dad inside.
He only wants to hear the radio.

Bad handbrake, and a diesel, someone said.
Ignition on, it lurches into you
and the boy's so scared he just accelerates.
The silence he escaped is breaking through.
For the want of radio, you're left for dead.

All those cars that almost knocked you down:
it had to be this one in a resort
by the Phuket sea, with snorkelling and sun
and caves that you were planning to explore –
but you'd rather die in Thailand than in town.

You nearly didn't go on holiday:
afraid for your husband's health, some nagging pain
that might be kidney stones. Who told you, *Go*?
I hope it wasn't me – it could have been –
that left me motherless, and miles away.

This is your legacy: dry skin. Green gaze.
A neck that's prone to cricking. Heavy bones.
Babies that come out blond. A love of numbers.

Particular loud, enthusiastic tones.
The hard-wired knack to utter turns of phrase

that knock our loved ones senseless: thoughtless truths
like paper darts that turn, mid-air, to stones.
I know you never meant to hurt me, Mum:
without my dad, I'd swear we must be clones.
I pigeon-hole my kids as much as you.

I've half become the mum I can't condemn
who tells me on my wedding day, sincere,
You're the most beautiful woman in the room.
Except your sister. Baffled by my tears.
The make-up lady has to start again.

As we would start again, in better times.
Show me a mother whose daughter doesn't bleed.
Who didn't grow up clinging to *her* mother,
an endless irritation of her knees –
which drives the child to excellence, to shine,

and drives her, as a mum, to disappear,
to pin, and run up at night, slit-to-the-waist
gold lamé dresses, Lurex. A 'notice me'
that comes from being small; and what's good taste
is jettisoned like sandbags in the fear

that you might crash unnoticed into truth.
When love's at stake, it's better to be blind;
my perfect childhood was a work of fiction.
My father gave me my enquiring mind;
the brutal honesty, I got from you.

But I wouldn't be myself without your gifts.
And it's against your warp I weave this story,
consistent as a windsock in a whirlwind.
At least, you said to me, *I'm never boring.*
So now I've summoned you, I'll tell you this.

This is your story. Beauty needs its flaws.
The speed-bump potholes of the unmade road
beside deserted beach and postcard sea
would stop you reaching hospital. You'd go
from the man you loved, his hand enclosing yours.

It's like the moon, the lovers' cheesy cross:
you wouldn't want it smooth, or vastly bigger.
A faster road would not have been romantic
and might have brought you moments to consider;
and who wants to consider every loss?

There was a girl, once, with a lazy eye,
unable to judge distances, or speeds,
who got through sixty-six long years despite
that lurching half of the world she couldn't see.
With accidents, you had an alibi.

But a moment's blindness was a lifetime trait.
I sat in your blind side every other day
and learnt to fill the gaps instinctively:
the focused lens you couldn't wish away,
the damaged daughter who would tell it straight.

An accident. Abrupt, untidy end.
Still, the motif of radio recurs
as if it were a way of tuning in
to private services for the disturbed:
the word as blessing, salve, and sacrament.

Some recent poetry from Anvil

MICHAEL ALEXANDER
Old English Riddles

KATERINA ANGHELAKI-ROOKE
The Scattered Papers of Penelope
Edited by Karen Van Dyck

NINA CASSIAN
Continuum

TOM DISCH
About the Size of It

MICHAEL HAMBURGER
Circling the Square

JAMES HARPUR
The Dark Age
Boethius: *Fortune's Prisoner*

DAVID HINTON
Mountain Home

GABRIEL LEVIN
The Maltese Dreambook

MATTHEW MEAD
The Autumn-Born in Autumn

DENNIS O'DRISCOLL
Reality Check

GRETA STODDART
Salvation Jane

RABINDRANATH TAGORE
The Golden Boat
Translated by Joe Winter

PAUL VALÉRY
Charms
Translated by Peter Dale